*Hero or Villain?*

Claims and Counterclaims

# Christopher Columbus

## Controversial Explorer of the Americas

Christopher C. Brink

D0898775

Cavendish Square

New York

Published in 2019 by Cavendish Square Publishing, LLC
243 5th Avenue, Suite 136, New York, NY 10016

Library of Congress Cataloging-in-Publication Data

Names: Brink, Christopher, author.
Title: Christopher Columbus : controversial explorer of the Americas / Christopher Brink.
Description: First edition. | New York : Cavendish Square, 2019. | Series: Hero or villain? Claims and counterclaims | Includes bibliographical references and index. | Audience: Grades 7-12.
Identifiers: LCCN 2017052049 (print) | LCCN 2017052780 (ebook) | ISBN 9781502635235 (library bound) | ISBN 9781502635259 (pbk.) | ISBN 9781502635242 (ebook)
Subjects: LCSH: Columbus, Christopher--Juvenile literature. | Explorers--America--Biography--Juvenile literature. | Explorers--Spain--Biography--Juvenile literature. | America--Discovery and exploration--Spanish--Juvenile literature.
Classification: LCC E111 (ebook) | LCC E111 .B86 2019 (print) | DDC 970.01/5092 [B] --dc23
LC record available at https://lccn.loc.gov/2017052049

Editorial Director: David McNamara
Editor: Michael Spitz
Copy Editor: Rebecca Rohan
Associate Art Director: Amy Greenan
Designer: Amy Greenan/Christina Shults
Production Coordinator: Karol Szymczuk
Photo Research: J8 Media

The photographs in this book are used by permission and through the courtesy of:
Chapter openers, Anonymous Portuguese (1502)/Biblioteca Estense Universitaria, Modena, Italy/Wikimedia Commons/File: Cantino planisphere (1502).jpg/Public Domain; p. 4 / Gift of J. Pierpont Morgan, 1900/Metropolitan Museum of Art, online collection/Wikimedia Commons/File: Portrait of a Man, Said to be Christopher Columbus.jpg/Public Domain; p. 6 Heinrich Hammer/Beinecke Library, Yale University/Wikimedia Commons/File: Martellus-Yale.jpg/Public Domain; p. 7 Charles Phelps Cushing/Classic Stock/Getty Images; p. 11 Mindriot/Wikimedia Commons/File: Conceptions Colomb map-en.svg/CCA-SA 3.0 Unported; p. 12 Rich Lynch/Shutterstock.com; pp. 16-17 Berthold Werner/Wikimedia Commons/File: Alexander and Bucephalus - Battle of Issus mosaic - Museo Archeologico Nazionale - Naples BW.jpg/CCA-SA 3.0 Unported; p. 21 William Murphy (http://flickr.com/photos/80824546@N00)/Wikimedia Commons/File: Viking Longship "Sea Stallion" Arrives in Dublin.jpg/CCA-SA 2.0 Generic; p. 26 Leemage/Hulton Fine Art Collection/Getty Images; p. 31 Michel Baudier/Wikimedia Commons/File: Mohammed MichelBaudier.jpg/Public Domain; pp. 36, 89 G. Dagli Orti/De Agostini Picture Library/Getty Images; p. 41 Print Collector/Hulton Archive/Getty Images; p. 44 Columbus_before_the Queen, Brooklyn Museum/Wikimedia Commons/File: Emanuel Gottlieb Leutze - Columbus Before the Queen.jpg/Public Domain; p. 47 Photo scan (Book: Historia del Arte) Wikimedia Commons/File: Desembarco de Colón de Dióscoro Puebla.jpg/Public Domain; p. 50 Leemage/UIG/Getty Images; p. 51 Eugene Delacroix/Wikimedia Commons/File: WC Delacroix, Eugene The Return of Christopher Columbus.jpg/Public Domain; p. 58 Stock Montage/Getty Images; p. 61 UIG/Getty Images; p. 67 KVDP/Wikimedia Commons/File: Map prevailing winds on earth.png/Public Domain; p. 70 Camille Flammarion/Wikimedia Commons/File: Eclipse Christophe Colomb.jpg/Public Domain; p. 72 Wikimedia Commons /File: Amerigo Vespucci.jpg/Public Domain; pp. 83, 91 A. Dagli Orti/De Agostini Picture Library/Getty Images; p. 84 3LH/SuperStock; p. 87 Stock Montage/Getty Images; p. 95 Visions of America/UIG/Getty Images; p. 98 Paul Fearn/Alamy Stock Photo.

Printed in the United States of America

# CON TENTS

Portrait of a Man, Said to be *Christopher Columbus* by Sebastiano del Piombo.

# Who Was Christopher Columbus?

## Chapter One

C hristopher Columbus was an explorer of Italian descent who has gotten credit for discovering the area of the world now known as the Western Hemisphere. This includes the continents of North America and South America, as well as numerous neighboring islands. Prior to his initial voyage in 1492, Europeans generally believed that the Ocean Sea (now known as the Atlantic Ocean) extended uninterrupted to the east coast of Asia, or the Indies.

Columbus lived in a time when European monarchs were seeking to expand their empires quickly and significantly. Inland trade routes had been established across the continent of Asia, allowing for the exchange of goods between eastern Asia and Europe. Traveling through the mountainous

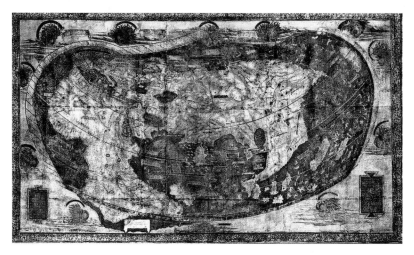

A map of the known world in Columbus's time.

terrain was very difficult and dangerous, however. This was further complicated by the rapid expansion of the Turkish Empire, whose people aggressively sought to take over the world, slaughtering all who stood in their path.

Advances in navigation and shipbuilding were allowing for further oceanic exploration than had been possible up to that point. Columbus took a great interest in these endeavors at a young age. He was particularly fascinated by cartography and often studied maps as well as the writings of the explorers who predated him, such as Marco Polo, who had been instrumental in developing a land route across Asia in the thirteenth century. Columbus gradually developed a theory that it would be possible to reach the Indies by sailing west across the ocean, thus allowing for safe trade with the people of this area, who possessed spices and other goods deemed valuable in Europe at the time.

Columbus makes his proposal to King Ferdinand and Queen Isabella of Spain.

Columbus initially attempted to gain support for his idea from King John II of Portugal. When this proved unsuccessful, he met with Queen Isabella and King Ferdinand of Spain, who agreed to be his patrons and supply him with ships and a crew for his travels. He set sail on his initial journey in 1492 and ultimately landed on an island in the modern-day Bahamas, which he claimed for Spain and named "San Salvador." He spent several months in this area before returning to Spain, accompanied by several natives of the area, whom he called "Indios," as he claimed that he had reached India.

Columbus and his crew set up a colony on the island as well as other nearby islands at this point and began exchanging goods with the indigenous peoples. He returned to Spain shortly afterward and was triumphantly received by the king and queen, who were pleased with his apparently successful endeavor. They bestowed upon him the title of "Admiral of the Ocean Sea" and commissioned a second voyage to the colony he had claimed, granting him the title of governor of the new settlement upon his return.

Columbus's next voyage led him to explore additional islands in the area. He named several of them, including Dominica, Marie-Galante, and Guadeloupe, and claimed them for Spain as well. During this time, he also named the Virgin Islands and explored the island now known as Puerto Rico.

A third voyage was undertaken in 1498, after news had spread of the believed existence of an unexplored continent to the southwest of the area that Columbus had explored.

# Other Important Explorers

**Leif Eriksson** An explorer of Norwegian descent, believed to have been the first person from Europe to set foot on the continent of North America when he landed in what is now called Newfoundland in the eleventh century.

**Marco Polo** An Italian merchant who lived in the late thirteenth and early fourteenth centuries. He traveled a great distance by land across Asia. He is credited with the development of the initial trade routes with China and the Indies.

**Vasco da Gama** A Portuguese explorer who lived in the late fifteenth and early sixteenth centuries, who has been credited with being the first person to actually arrive at India by sea.

Columbus and his crew landed at Trinidad and shortly thereafter discovered the mainland of South America. They explored the northern part of the continent, including modern Venezuela.

Prior to returning to Spain, Columbus went to Hispaniola, the colony he had originally founded. He discovered that a rebellion had been organized among the colonists, many of whom felt that he was an inept and tyrannical governor. This situation was compounded by the fact that word had reached Spain of the settlers' disdain for Columbus. A new governor was sent to the colony, and Columbus was arrested and brought back to Spain in chains. He was brought before Ferdinand and Isabella and convinced them to free him. He was unable to regain his title of governor of Hispaniola, however.

In 1502, Columbus undertook his fourth and final voyage to the New World. He initially intended to explore more new lands, but he became aware of an impending hurricane and sailed for Hispaniola to seek shelter. The new governor refused to allow him to land, ignored his warning regarding the storm, and sent thirty ships for Spain with gold. This fleet was almost completely wiped out by the hurricane, with only one ship surviving.

After the passing of the storm, which inflicted minimal damage on Columbus's own ships, he explored parts of Central America, including modern Nicaragua, Costa Rica, Honduras, and Panama. He eventually encountered another sizable storm that caused significant damage to his ships. They arrived in Jamaica, where they spent approximately

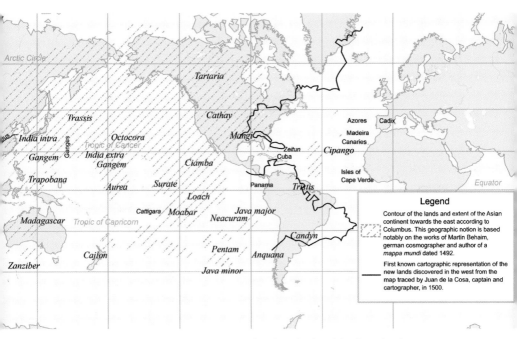

Columbus explored many new territories during his time in the Western Hemisphere.

one year among the natives before finally being rescued and returning to Spain.

Throughout the past five hundred years, Columbus's voyages have significantly impacted societies and cultures all over the world. Despite the fact that he never attained his initial goal of reaching Southeast Asia, his endeavors are often said to be successful in that they ultimately resulted in many benefits for Spain. However, there has been much disagreement among historians as to whether Columbus should be considered a hero or a villain.

The ruins of the Parthenon demonstrate the architectural skill of the ancient Greeks.

# History of Europe Before Columbus

## Chapter Two

The world into which Christopher Columbus was born was highly imperialistic. European countries competed with one another for land, goods, and status. New methods of shipbuilding were being developed at a fast pace, and traders were advancing farther around the world than ever before in search of profitable goods. Colonies were being developed along the coast of Africa, and some countries began imprisoning the natives from this area and transporting them to Europe, where they were sold into slavery. In order to understand how this competitive atmosphere developed, it is important to examine European history prior to the birth of Columbus.

# Early European Cultures

One of the earliest known organized civilizations in Europe was that of ancient Greeks, also known as the Mycenaeans. Records indicate that this society developed around the twelfth century BCE. The Greeks of this era communicated through a written and spoken language and expressed themselves through primitive art work. The Mycenaeans' culture collapsed around the eleventh century BCE; they were overtaken by outsiders from the eastern Mediterranean Sea, as famine in their native lands forced them to seek out new food sources and goods.

By the fourth century BCE, Greece began to flourish once again. A monarchy had been established, and Alexander III of Macedon became king. He would become known as Alexander the Great, due to his success in expanding the Greek territory during his reign. He developed a strong military, which would prove undefeatable in battle. At the time of his death in 323 BCE, the Greek empire had spread into northeastern Africa and into Asia as far as India.

Society in Greece continued to develop as advances were made in architecture, artwork, and philosophy. The remaining ruins of buildings, such as the Parthenon, demonstrate the highly organized nature of the Greeks and the degree to which they valued aesthetic appearances.

The Greeks of this time are credited with being the first society to begin to carefully record their history. Herodotus, who maintained several written accounts of the lives and acts of a variety of historical figures, is regarded as the first known true historian. Many others, including Thucydides,

Demosthenes, and Xenophon, followed in his footsteps, providing fairly detailed records of the progress and development of their society.

The field of philosophy began to develop in Greece during this time as well. Pythagoras, who lived from 570 to 495 BCE, made great advances in the understanding of the world through mathematics. The philosopher Plato (428 BCE to 347 BCE) expressed the belief that all objects in the visible world were imperfect copies of their ideal forms, or archetypes, and that the development of reason in the mind of a person could allow for the perception of the perfect world. Aristotle (384 BCE to 322 BCE), a student of Plato, wrote on many subjects, including physics, poetry, music, logic, and ethics.

## Rome

The civilization of Rome would ultimately overtake Greece in terms of economic and cultural development as well as expansion. Beginning in the eighth century BCE, the inhabitants of the area quickly built up a large city, from which they rapidly expanded outward. It would ultimately encompass approximately 2 million square miles (5 million square kilometers) in total area.

The ancient Romans were responsible for further significant advances in technology and architecture. They developed roads throughout their territory, resulting in fairly easy and safe travel. Furthermore, they created an intricate series of aqueducts to allow quick movement of water throughout their lands. This improved farming and allowed for the development of public baths and decorative fountains.

Alexander the Great was highly regarded for his skill in battle.

A unique aspect of the early Roman civilization was their system of government. Now referred to as a republic, it placed emphasis on the common good and sought to provide a cooperative way of life, which valued all of its people. This would prove to be the ultimate basis for future democratic societies, including the United States.

Beginning in 92 BCE, Rome went to war with Parthia, beginning a period of conflict known as the Roman-Persian Wars, which would ultimately last 721 years. Due to the violence of this period, Roman culture changed significantly, as a more imperialistic atmosphere became prevalent. Ultimately, Rome became a dictatorship under Augustus Caesar, who ruled from 27 BCE to 14 CE. He developed an enormous army and began a campaign with the ultimate goal of taking over the world. During his lifetime, the Roman Empire would extend throughout modern Europe, as well as the northern coast of Africa.

The Roman Empire continued to be the dominant culture of Europe until 476 CE. At this point, a number of factors are regarded as responsible for its fall. The size of the empire made it difficult to effectively govern, as outside barbarian cultures were beginning to fight against it on multiple fronts. The size of the army had declined over the years, and it was no longer able to effectively defend the full territory. Civil unrest within the empire also led to a good deal of infighting among its people. Historians attribute the fall of the Roman Empire to inept leadership at this time, as well.

# The Middle Age

The dissolution of the Roman Empire marked the beginning of the historical era known as the Middle Ages. During this time, many new kingdoms were developed in the western part of the former empire, now known as Europe. The Christian religion became widely accepted in the initial European cultures, particularly among the Franks, who established the short-lived Carolingian Empire and began to develop monasteries throughout the area. This was the predominant culture of Europe through the early ninth century, but it fell apart due to invasions by the Vikings and other barbaric peoples from the surrounding regions.

Around the year 1000 CE, the system of feudalism became commonplace. Under this system, wealthy noblemen who owned land would rent portions of their land to knights in return for military service. Fighting among nobles and the knights who owed allegiance to them was commonplace during this time. Gradually, monarchies began to arise, resulting in a general decline in violence.

As Catholicism was spreading in Europe during the Middle Ages, the Catholic Holy Land east of the Mediterranean Sea had come under the control of the Turkish practitioners of Islam, a rival religion. Pope Urban II organized the First Crusade in 1095 in an attempt to regain control of the Holy Land by force. Many European knights and peasants volunteered to fight against the Turks in this and six subsequent Crusades, either as a means of showing their devotion to God or to attain political and economic status. Ultimately, the Crusades proved unsuccessful in regaining the Holy Land. By 1291, this goal was all but abandoned.

The remainder of the Middle Ages proved to be a dark time in which the overall population of Europe dropped significantly. A plague known as the Black Death swept through the area in the middle of the fourteenth century, killing millions of people. This, along with widespread famine, made life bleak for those who survived. Violence increased within kingdoms once again as peasants, unhappy with their current state of affairs, revolted against their leaders.

## The Vikings

The early inhabitants of Northern Europe, or Scandinavia, were known as Vikings. They were a seafaring people who began exploring and settling in other areas starting in the eighth century CE. They have been depicted as violent and bloodthirsty, brutally attacking the inhabitants of the lands they sought to take over. It is widely believed among historians that the Vikings intended to expand outward due to a rapid increase in population in an area that could support limited agriculture. Under these circumstances, many Scandinavian inhabitants would have grown desperate for property and wealth, ultimately resorting to piracy.

The Vikings were aided in their travels by the invention of the longship. This wooden ship, with sails made from woven wool, was the result of many years' worth of innovation and was characterized by the ability to navigate

A modern replica of a Viking longship

very shallow waters. It was very lightweight, which allowed it to be easily carried if necessary. A further advantage of the longship was its "double-ended" shape. Both ends were shaped identically, which allowed for a quick reversal in direction.

## Arrival in North America

While the Vikings were seeking to expand southward into Europe, some also began to venture westward through the Atlantic Ocean. One of the earliest of such journeys is credited to Erik the Red. Originally an inhabitant of Iceland, he was banished for three years as a punishment

# Timeline of European History Prior to Columbus

**1100s BCE**  Development of ancient Greek civilization commences.

**700s BCE**  Greek colonization of surrounding areas begins. Rome begins to develop.

**400s BCE**  Greco-Persian Wars begin.

**336 BCE**  Alexander the Great assumes control of Greece.

**323 BCE**  Death of Alexander the Great.

**92 BCE**  Roman-Persian Wars begin.

**476 CE**  Fall of the Roman Empire and beginning of the Middle Ages.

**701–800**  Vikings begin outward expansion.

**985**  Bjarni Herjulfsson spots North American mainland.

| | |
|---|---|
| **1001** | Leif Eriksson arrives at Newfoundland. |
| **1004** | Norsemen abandon first North American settlement. |
| **1001–1100** | Feudalism develops in most of Europe. |
| **1095** | Pope Urban II organizes First Crusade. |
| **1271** | Marco Polo begins traveling across Europe and Asia. |
| **1291** | The Crusades end. |
| **1295** | Marco Polo returns home to Venice. |
| **1346** | Black Death begins to spread across Europe. |

for manslaughter. He sailed westward and landed at a hitherto unexplored landmass, which he subsequently named "Greenland" as part of his plan to attract settlers there (he assumed this name would sound enticing). He did, in fact, convince a number of followers to settle there, establishing its first colony.

In 985 CE, shortly after the colonization of Greenland, the first European sighting of the North American mainland occurred, quite accidentally. Bjarni Herjulfsson, a merchant sailing en route to Greenland from Iceland, encountered turbulent weather and was separated from his fleet. He sailed in isolation for three days and spotted land to the west. He was not interested in exploring a new area and quickly found his way to his intended destination. He recounted his sighting of the land to Leif Eriksson, son of Erik the Red, who was excited by the prospect of establishing a new settlement.

Eriksson eventually landed in what is now Newfoundland, which he named Vinland, becoming the first European to set foot in North America. He spent the winter there in 1001 and remained there for another year, but shortly thereafter returned to Greenland. His brother Thorvald sailed to his camp in 1004, accompanied by thirty men. He and his men attacked a group of nine natives. They killed eight of them, but the ninth escaped and quickly retaliated against Thorvald with a larger group. Thorvald was killed in the subsequent conflict. The surviving Norsemen left shortly afterward, bringing an end to this first North American settlement.

# Marco Polo

Marco Polo was a merchant from Venice who traveled extensively throughout Asia and established trade routes between Europe and the Orient. He carefully recorded details of his travels and was instrumental in the introduction of Eastern and Western cultures to one another.

In 1271, at the age of seventeen, he embarked on his journey through Asia in the company of his father and uncle. His travels lasted a total of twenty-four years, during which time he amassed great wealth. Upon his return home, he found that Venice was engaged in war with Genoa. He joined the war and was subsequently captured and imprisoned by the Genoese.

While in prison, Polo passed the time recounting his travels in great detail to another prisoner named Rustichello da Pisa, who recorded the stories in writing. The written account was published as *The Travels of Marco Polo*, which would be widely read throughout Europe. This generated a significant interest in the cultures of China, Japan, and India, all of which had been visited by Polo during his travels.

## Travels

Prior to Marco Polo leaving Venice, his father Niccolo and uncle Maffeo had made a journey across Asia and ultimately arrived in China in 1266, where they met Kublai Khan in Dadu, which is now known as Beijing. Khan had never encountered Europeans prior to their arrival and was fascinated by their accounts of the European political and

Marco Polo was a pioneer in exploration. He greatly inspired Columbus.

economic systems. Khan took a keen interest in Christianity and asked Niccolo and Maffeo to bring a letter to Pope Clement IV, requesting that a group of Christians be sent to teach him about their ways of life. They returned to Venice to find that the pope had died and that a successor was yet to be named. At this point, they remained in Venice for a year in anticipation of the selection of the next pope.

Young Marco was enthusiastic about traveling and joined Niccolo and Maffeo on their journey back to Kublai Khan. They left Venice in 1271 by ship and sailed to the port of Acre, in Israel. They then headed toward China by way of the Silk Road (a trade route which led from the Mediterranean Sea to Korea). While traveling with a caravan of merchants in the desert, they were set upon by bandits in a sandstorm. Most of the party was killed, but the Polos were able to escape and continue on their path.

The Polos finally arrived at the palace of Shangdu, where Kublai Khan welcomed them. He was particularly fascinated by Marco's ability to speak multiple languages. Marco and his father and uncle remained in China for several years, during which time Marco traveled extensively around the kingdom. When the Polos indicated that they were ready to leave China to return home, Khan refused to allow them to do so.

In 1292, the Polos were finally allowed to leave the country when the ruler of Persia, a relative of Kublai Khan, sent his representatives to China with instructions to find a wife for him. Khan sent Marco, Niccolo, and Maffeo to accompany the selected bride. They embarked on a two-year sea voyage, ultimately landing at Hormuz. From there, they parted company with their fellow travelers and headed home.

Marco Polo's accounts of his travels had a major impact on world exploration beyond his lifetime. Cartographers, or mapmakers, updated world maps to a great extent based on his descriptions of Asia and the Orient. Interestingly, Polo never endeavored to create a map himself. His three daughters and other descendants designed several of them, which contain fairly accurate representations of Japan and the eastern coast of Asia, from which travel routes were developed by many later explorers, including Columbus.

# The Spread of Christianity

In order to fully understand the European culture into which Columbus was born, the influence of Christianity must be taken into account. By the time of his birth, the influence of the Catholic Church had become widespread throughout the "civilized" world. Many practitioners of the religion saw it as their mission to spread the teachings of the Holy Bible to unenlightened people. These teachers would become known as missionaries. The goal of spreading Christianity, or Christianization, proved to be a major motivator for travel to, and exploration of, new areas of the world.

## Christianization of Northern Europe

Christianity began to spread into Central and Northern Europe early in the Middle Ages. The Germanic people who inhabited this area had historically worshiped pagan gods such as Thor. When they were first made aware of the biblical concept of Christ, they initially assimilated it into their pagan belief system. It became fairly common for those heading into war to pray to Jesus as well as pagan gods, in the hope that they would be granted more of an advantage over their enemies.

The Anglo-Saxon inhabitants of the area, now known as England, gradually accepted Christianity, mainly as a result of a group of missionaries being sent there by Pope Gregory I in the year 596.

The leader of this group was Augustine of Canterbury. They first met with the royal family, who willingly converted to the new religion. In short order, Christianity had spread throughout the kingdom.

Around this time, Christian monasteries were being established in Ireland. One unique characteristic of the Irish monks was their common decision to "punish" themselves for their sins by self-imposed exile to heathen lands. Upon arrival, they would attempt to convert the native people to Christianity as a means of penance, with the hope of redemption in the afterlife.

The nation of Poland was developed largely as a result of the introduction of Catholicism. In 966, an inhabitant named Mieszko was baptized, thereby becoming a Catholic. Backed by the support of the church, he unified the people of the area and ultimately became the nation's first king.

Hungary underwent a gradual Christianization beginning in 950. At the time, the Magyar tribes inhabited the land. A highly respected chief named Gyula was baptized at Constantinople. Eventually, his grandson Stephen became ruler of the land. He was appointed King by Pope Sylvester II and established Christianity as the national religion.

He would be granted sainthood by the Catholic Church approximately fifty years after his death for his evangelical efforts and support of the Crusades.

Christianization began in Scandinavia when missionaries arrived in Denmark in the eighth century. The people of this area were very resistant to changing their beliefs. As a result, conversion took much longer here than in other areas of Europe. Historians estimate that most inhabitants of the Scandinavian nations had accepted Christianity by the twelfth century, although some continued to worship the gods of Norse traditions for several hundred years afterward.

# The Spread of Islam

The religion of Islam, whose practitioners are known as Muslims, was quickly developing in the lands to the east of the Mediterranean Sea during the Middle Ages. The difference in beliefs between Muslims and Christians was a source of significant, often violent conflict during this time. The strife caused by this conflict had a significant cultural and economic impact on Europe and would ultimately prove to be a major motivator for Columbus to seek a new sea route to the Orient.

## Origin of Islam

The religion of Islam was started by Muhammad (570–632), a self-proclaimed prophet from Mecca who began reporting revelations from God in the year 610. His revelations were organized in written form and became the Quran, or holy

La naiſſance, la vie, & la mort de Mahomet,
impoſteur abominable, & faux Prophete des
Turcs, Mores, Arabes, Egyptiens, Perſes,
Tartares, & quelques Indiens.

## CHAP. II.

Evx rares hommes de l'antiquité diſcourans de
l'ambition, & de l'ambitieux, depeignoient par
leurs parolles la verité de tous les deux: car l'vn
diſoit de celle-là, qu'elle eſtoit la baſe ſur laquelle ſap-

The prophet Muhammad, founder of the religion of Islam

book of Islam. Muhammad began preaching in Mecca against the predominantly polytheistic tradition of worshipping multiple gods and won over a small group of supporters. They soon became the subject of persecution, as the ruling class of Mecca concluded that Muhammad was attempting to undermine their authority by introducing the concept of equality among all people.

Following twelve years of persecution in Mecca, Muhammad and his followers eventually moved to Medina in the year 622. In Medina, Muhammad was finally accepted by the majority of inhabitants. He established the Constitution of Medina, which listed rights and laws intended to protect all people, regardless of religion. One major tenet of the constitution was the declaration that Medina was sacred and was to be free of violence.

Medina remained a peaceful and harmonious community until 624, when the Meccans attacked Medina in the Battle of Badr. The Muslims successfully fought the Meccans off at this point. In 625, the Meccans returned to fight them in the Battle of Uhud. Many lives were lost on both sides, and there was no clear victor.

The Battle of the Trench followed in 627, in which a number of Arab tribes attacked the Muslims at Medina. This skirmish lasted until the following year, when peace between Mecca and Medina was temporarily established by the Treaty of Hudaybiyyah. Muhammad attained many more followers afterward, and the Muslims returned to Mecca in 629, where they easily established control of the city. Muhammad passed away in 632, having united all of Arabia under the tenets of Islam.

## The Ottoman Empire

After several centuries during which Islam continued to spread and develop, the Ottoman Empire was established in Turkey. By the thirteenth century, the area consisted of several independent tribes called beyliks. One beylik leader, known as Osman, began to conquer neighboring areas with an army of Islamic followers.

When Osman died in 1324, his son Orhan became leader of the territory, which was now known as Ottoman. Orhan continued to expand his territory into Anatolia, ultimately taking over Bursa, which he established as the Ottoman capital. The Ottomans took over the Serbian city of Kosovo in 1389. At this point, they were poised to expand into Europe. The last of the Crusades in 1396 proved unsuccessful in defeating the Ottomans.

The Ottomans suffered a rare setback after the Battle of Ankara, which took place in 1402. By this point, the Ottoman Sultan (or leader) was Bayezid I. He was taken prisoner by forces led by Timur. An internal war ensued, due to disagreement over which of Bayezid's sons should succeed him in authority. Eventually, a new sultan, Mehmed I, was established, bringing an end to the conflict and reuniting the Ottomans.

The Ottoman territory continued to grow throughout the early fifteenth century. Sultan Murad II was victorious over Poland in the Battle of Varna in 1444. A further attempt was made to defeat the Turks at Kosovo in 1448, this time by Hungary. Murad II once again emerged as the victor.

The ultimate goal of the Ottomans was the takeover of Constantinople, then capital of the Byzantine Empire, which had evolved from the Roman Empire. Sultan Mehmed, son of Murad II, had succeeded his father and led an attack on Constantinople on April 6, 1453. The siege continued until May 29, at which point the city was surrendered to the Ottomans.

Constantinople was quickly established as the new capital of the Ottoman Empire. This essentially ended the Byzantine Empire and put the Ottomans in a favorable position to expand into Europe. After the takeover, Mehmed allowed the Greek Orthodox Church within the city to remain, provided that its leaders acknowledge the political authority of the Ottomans.

In 1460, the Ottomans invaded Morea, one of the few remaining Byzantine territories. They took over Byzantine-ruled Trebizond the following year. At this time, the Europeans were becoming increasingly wary of the potential threat of Muslim invasion. When word of the fall of Constantinople reached Pope Nicholas V, he attempted to organize a crusade to regain Catholic control of the city. This was unsuccessful, as European rulers were too intimidated by the size and aggressive nature of the Ottoman military to engage in such an attack.

Ultimately, the Albanians were able to temporarily fend off Turkish expansion into Eastern Europe under the skilled leadership of George Castriot. The Ottomans attempted several times to invade Albania over a period of approximately twenty-five years in the mid-fifteenth century, but they were repeatedly repelled by Castriot and his military forces. In 1479, the Turks finally defeated the Albanians with the takeover of the city of Shkodra.

## Effects on European Economy

As of the late fifteenth century, the rapid growth and increase in power of the Ottoman Empire was presenting a significant problem for Europeans. The Turks were working to gain control of a sizable territory between Europe and the Orient. In the past, European merchants had been able to safely travel to and from the Indies by way of the Silk Road. Passage was now far more dangerous due to the risk of attack by hostile Turks.

The threat that the Ottoman Empire posed to trade between Europe and East Asia created an economic dilemma, due to the value of goods such as silk and spices from China and the Indies. These were in great demand among Europeans. The increased difficulty with overland travel, combined with the advances being made in shipbuilding and navigation, would soon lead to consideration of a potential alternative trade route by sea.

Columbus and his crew benefited from rapid advances in shipbuilding.

# The Life of Columbus

## Chapter Three

**D**etails about the birth of Christopher Columbus are scarce, due to poor record-keeping at the time. As indicated by John Dyson in his book *Columbus: For Gold, God, and Glory,* it is generally accepted that Columbus was born in Genoa, Italy. His exact lineage is questionable. While regarded as Italian throughout history, there has been recent speculation that he may have been of Greek descent. The exact date of his birth is also unknown but is estimated to have been sometime in the autumn of 1451. His Italian birth name was Cristoforo, and he reportedly took great pride in sharing the name of the patron saint of travelers.

## Early Life

Columbus was one of five children born to Domenico Colombo and Susanna Fontanarossa. He had three brothers (Bartolomeo, Giovanni, and Giacomo) and one sister (Bianchinetta). Domenico made his living by operating a wool-weaving business in Genoa, into which he enlisted the help of his children.

When Columbus was a child, Genoese society was turbulent and characterized by violence. Attacks from foreign rivals, including the Ottoman Turks, were commonplace due to Genoa's proximity to the Mediterranean Sea. Adding to the tension was a good deal of fighting among the residents of Genoa. Members of rival families frequently attacked one another in the streets, and a close friend of Columbus's father was stoned to death, according to John Dyson in *Columbus: For Gold, God, and Glory*. Columbus himself would attribute his development of "street smarts" to growing up under these circumstances.

Columbus received virtually no formal education due to the demands of his father's business when he was young. As a result, he was illiterate for most of his early life. Working for his father taught him a strong work ethic, which would serve him well throughout his life. He found the wool-weaving business to be boring and monotonous, however, and dreamed of traveling and pursuing a more adventurous way of life.

When Columbus had free time as a boy, he would often venture to the Genoese harbor , where he became fascinated by the merchant ships that he saw. Although he did not receive a traditional education, he was a keen observer, paid close attention to the conversations he overheard among sailors, and gradually acquired a rudimentary knowledge of ship maintenance and navigation. He also took note of the gold and slaves frequently brought back from Africa aboard many returning ships and thus developed a desire for economic success.

## Early Adventures in Sailing

It is estimated that Columbus left his father's business at the age of fourteen to become a sailor. He embarked on his first voyage in either 1474 or 1475 on a ship that was part of a convoy headed east through the Mediterranean Sea. Reports had been made that Genoese merchants on the Greek island of Chios were soon to be threatened by the Turks, and the convoy's mission was to defend or rescue the merchants. When the ships arrived at their destination, it was determined that there was no actual threat, so they quickly returned home. Despite the relative lack of excitement of this initial voyage, Columbus took note of the fact that the Turks had made the traditional route to the Far East virtually impenetrable.

Columbus embarked on his second voyage on May 31, 1476. This time, he was part of a convoy of merchants destined for northern Europe. He docked in the English port of Bristol and later in Ireland. It has been speculated that he may have traveled as far as Iceland during this time, but this cannot be verified. In any event, Columbus continued to gain valuable experience in sailing and greatly enjoyed visiting foreign lands.

In late 1477, the convoy headed back to Genoa. When it reached Cape Saint Vincent on the edge of southern Portugal, the ships were attacked by a massive fleet of French and Portuguese war ships. A lengthy battle ensued, during which most of the Genoese ships were destroyed and a great number of lives were lost. Columbus was reportedly thrown from his ship into the water and kept himself afloat by clinging to an oar until the fighting ended. He then headed for shore and made it to land several hours later.

Columbus traveled through Portugal at this time. He arrived in Lisbon, where he eventually located his brother Bartolomeo, who was working there as a cartographer. He settled in Lisbon and went into business with his brother, quickly learning the art of mapmaking. In the autumn of 1479, he married Felipa Moniz Perestrello. Shortly afterward, she bore him a son, Diego Columbus.

In 1482, Columbus sailed with a Portuguese convoy along the west coast of Africa, where he engaged in trading. He would not return to Portugal until 1485, when he received news that Felipa had died. Columbus then sailed for Castile (a region of Spain) with Diego. It was there, in 1487, that he met Beatriz Enriquez de Arana, who would become the mother of his second son. Fernando Columbus was born in July of 1488.

## Influences

Despite his lack of formal education, Columbus possessed a good deal of ambition and enjoyed learning. He learned multiple written languages, including Portuguese and Latin, which enabled him to study numerous books. He particularly

Sea battles in the late fifteenth century were chaotic and bloody.

loved *The Travels of Marco Polo* and *Historia Rerum Ubique Gestarum* by Pope Pius II. Through his studies, he became well versed in geography and astronomy, furthering his knowledge of navigation.

In addition to studying the sciences, Columbus took great interest in the Bible. A devout Catholic, he avidly studied the prophecies of the New Testament and developed the conviction that he had a duty to help spread the word of God. He would reference biblical verses in letters and journals throughout his life.

As Columbus studied the works of the great thinkers who had come before him, he became steadfast in the belief that the Indies could be reached by sailing west from Europe. This idea had been suggested by Paolo dal Pozzo Toscanelli, an astronomer from Florence, in 1470. Columbus found that the Greek philosopher Aristotle had made a similar claim approximately 1,800 years earlier. Through studying a treatise called *The Image of the World* by Cardinal Pierre d'Ailly, Columbus found that another Greek, Marinus of Tyre, had claimed in the second century CE that Asia could be reached by going west.

## Attempt to Gain Portuguese Patronage

King John II had become ruler of Portugal in 1481. In light of the Ottoman threats to overland trade, he professed a strong interest in finding a sea route to India. Columbus met with the king in 1484 and proposed the idea of sailing west to reach the east. The king agreed to carefully consider his proposal. A short time later, he rejected the plan, stating that he had met with experts who felt that Columbus had made major miscalculations. Columbus later learned that the king had secretly sent another sailor on a westward course, who had returned shortly afterward and reported that nothing had been found.

Columbus remained in Portugal and attempted to win support for his idea. Significant resources were being devoted to exploring Africa to the south, which would eventually result in the Portuguese explorer Bartolomeu Dias arriving at the Cape of Good Hope at the southernmost tip of the continent in 1488. Columbus soon concluded that his efforts to gain support from the Portuguese crown were futile.

## Success in Spain

After failing to convince the Portuguese ruler to support his idea, Columbus found himself in a state of depression. He was still mourning the loss of his wife and no longer felt at home in Portugal. Along with his son, he packed up his few belongings, bought a small vessel, and sailed eastward, eventually landing at the Spanish port of Andalusia. He sought lodging at a monastery, where he first met Fray Antonio de Marchena. Columbus spoke at great length with him about the idea of voyaging westward to arrive in the east, and the priest became an enthusiastic supporter of the idea. The priest soon introduced Columbus to the Duke of Medina Celi, who also agreed that his idea was worth serious consideration. The duke used his influence to arrange a meeting between Columbus and the Spanish monarchs, King Ferdinand and Queen Isabella.

After considerable effort, Columbus was granted the financial support he had sought from Ferdinand and Isabella

The Spanish monarchy found Columbus to be charming and charismatic.

in December of 1491. He was provided with three ships and a crew of ninety men for his voyage. Two of the ships, the *Niña* and the *Pinta*, were caravels, which had recently been developed by Portuguese shipbuilders specifically for lengthy sailing expeditions. They were lightweight and could attain higher speeds than other ships of the time. The third ship, the *Santa María*, was considerably larger and was captained by Columbus himself.

## First Voyage Across the Atlantic

Columbus and his crew departed Spain on August 3, 1492 from the port of Palos de la Frontera. They initially sailed southward to the Canary Islands, where they collected food,

# Columbus and the Spanish Crown

When Columbus first met with Ferdinand and Isabella, they reportedly found him charming and admired his enthusiasm and determination. They initially refused to sponsor his voyage after consulting with a group of advisors who felt that Columbus had underestimated the distance around the earth. Columbus followed the king and queen around Spain for several years, begging them to reconsider his proposal. Finally, the Spanish treasurer Luis de Santangel convinced them that Columbus's proposed voyage would cost very little, but that if another country sponsored him and he succeeded, it would be costly to Spain. When Columbus was notified that Ferdinand and Isabella would fund his voyage, he increased his demands. He stated that if he succeeded in reaching the Indies, in addition to payment, he wanted to be promoted to "Admiral of the Ocean Sea" as well as recognition as governor of any new territories he would claim for Spain. The king and queen ultimately agreed to all of his requests.

water, and other provisions. On September 6, they departed and began heading west. Several uneventful weeks passed, and the crew began to grow wary of Columbus. Some had heard rumors that giant sea monsters resided in unexplored areas of the ocean, while others feared that they would starve before finding land.

The circumstances under which land was first spotted have been a source of considerable debate. In the early morning of October 12, Juan Rodriguez Bermejo, a sailor aboard the *Pinta*, shouted that he had spotted land. The crew initially credited him with being the first to sight solid ground. Columbus quickly reported that he had seen moving light to the west of the ships the previous evening, however. In Columbus's own words, translated by scholar-author Robert Fuson, "It had the same appearance as a light or torch belonging to fishermen or travelers who alternately raised or lowered it, or perhaps were going from house to house. I now believe that the light I saw was a sign from God and that it was truly the first positive indication of land."

Prior to the voyage, Ferdinand and Isabella had promised that the first crew member to sight land would receive a lifelong pension. Bermejo, having been the first to make this declaration, believed that the pension was his. Columbus was ultimately awarded the pension due to his description of the light, despite not announcing it to anyone else until after Bermejo made his claim.

As the sun rose on the morning of October 12, Columbus and his crew stepped onto land. He named the island San

Columbus comes ashore and claims the land for Spain.

Salvador and immediately claimed it for Spain. Although it is known that this was an island in the modern Bahamas, exactly which island it was is unclear. In 1925, one such island was named San Salvador in the belief that it was where Columbus originally landed, but this cannot be verified.

The native people Columbus encountered appeared very peaceful, although he soon learned that they fought on occasion with tribes from neighboring islands who would sometimes come to try to take them captive. He noted from their primitive weapons that they would be easy for Europeans to overtake. Columbus referred to these people as Indios, as he still believed that he had landed somewhere near India. In a letter to the king and queen, he wrote that he would bring a small group of the Indios back to Spain to learn their culture.

## Further Exploration and Colonization

After staking claim to San Salvador, Columbus and his crew continued to explore other islands in the area, including modern Cuba. Having noted that some of the Indios wore earrings made of gold, they inquired as to where gold could be found in the region and continually searched for it. Martin Pinzon, a sailor among the crew, heard from a native that there was an island with a great deal of gold, which they called Babeque. Unbeknownst to Columbus, Pinzon commandeered the *Pinta* on November 22 and went in search of Babeque, not to be heard from for weeks. Columbus was angered by this but continued on in search of other new lands.

On December 5, Columbus arrived at the island that would come to be known as Hispaniola. The crew was well received by the inhabitants of the island. Their leader, Guacanagari, agreed to allow a contingent of thirty-nine men from Columbus's crew to remain on the island while Columbus made the return voyage to Spain. This did not occur as soon as Columbus had hoped. On December 24, the sailor manning the *Santa María* put an inexperienced deckhand in charge of steering the ship. In short order, it wrecked on a coral reef beyond repair. Columbus impressed the natives by firing cannons at its remains.

Columbus and his crew, minus the thirty-nine men who stayed behind, left Hispaniola aboard the *Niña* on January 4, 1493. Two days later, they crossed paths with Pinzon and the *Pinta*. Pinzon acknowledged that he had found no gold and apologized to Columbus, who welcomed him back. They made their final stop on January 13 at the Bay of Rincon on the northern coast of Hispaniola. Columbus attempted to trade cheap trinkets with the Ciguayo tribe for their bows and arrows. The negotiation took a negative turn, and there was a brief fight between the Ciguayos and the crew, after which Columbus took several of the Ciguayos prisoner. The captives were forced aboard the ships to be taken to Spain as slaves.

Not far into the return journey, the *Niña* and *Pinta* were separated by a violent storm. Columbus guided the *Niña* to the Azores, where they anchored at Santa Maria Island for the duration of the storm. When the weather cleared, several members of the crew went onto the island to praise God for keeping them safe through the turbulent weather. The island governor, assuming they were pirates, had them arrested. Columbus and the crew pleaded their case, and after two days, they were set free and continued toward home.

## Triumphant Return

After a brief stop in Portugal as the result of another storm, Columbus arrived at the port of Palos in Spain on March 13. Word of his accomplishment had already spread across Spain, and he was given a hero's welcome. As he traveled along the countryside en route to meet with Ferdinand and Isabella, hundreds of Spaniards stood along the road cheering him on.

The coat of arms awarded to Columbus upon his return to Spain.

*Christopher Columbus: Controversial Explorer of the Americas*

Columbus was given a hero's welcome when he returned from his first voyage.

The king and queen held a lavish celebration upon Columbus's arrival. In addition to a sizable monetary reward, he was given a house in Seville and his own coat of arms, which featured a lion and a castle. As requested, Columbus was also promoted to the rank of Admiral of the Ocean Sea and was recognized as viceroy, or governor, over the new lands that he had discovered and claimed for Spain.

## Later Voyages to the New World

Columbus was quickly tasked with a second voyage across the Atlantic to the lands, which were still believed to be near India. This time, he was granted a convoy of seventeen ships and approximately 1,200 men of a wide variety of occupations, with the intention of permanently colonizing the new Spanish territories. A number of priests were included, in keeping with Columbus's intent to spread Christianity among the natives.

## The Second Voyage

The convoy departed from Cadiz on September 24, 1493. They made their way to the Canary Islands to collect supplies and then began the trip across the ocean. Columbus chose to travel slightly farther south during this trip and first spotted land on November 3. He passed a number of islands that he named, such as Dominica, Santa Maria la Galante, and Les Saintes. He eventually went ashore on the island that he named Santa Maria de Guadalupe de Extremadura and spent a week exploring it. As he continued on his way, Columbus named a group of small islands Islas de Santa Ursula y las Once Mil Virgenas. They would come to be known as the Virgin Islands. The convoy then arrived at Puerto Rico, where the natives fought briefly with Columbus and his crew, forcing them to leave quickly.

Columbus eventually made his return to Hispaniola on November 22. He was surprised to find that his initial settlement (known as La Navidad) had been destroyed by the Indios and that eleven of the original men left behind had been killed. This was reportedly due to the men mistreating the natives and attempting to take their women as mistresses.

The final stop of this voyage was in the modern Dominican Republic. A settlement was established here, which Columbus named La Isabella, after the Spanish queen.

La Isabella did not last long, largely due to hurricanes in 1494 and 1495. The colonists who survived eventually became frustrated due to disease and lack of food. The settlement was ultimately abandoned in 1496.

## The Third Voyage

Columbus undertook a third voyage of exploration across the Atlantic in 1498. By this time, it had become accepted that the lands he had previously settled were not close to Asia, but Columbus still held out hope of finding passage to the Indies. Rumors of a full-size continent to the southwest had spread to King John II of Portugal at this point, and Columbus wanted to determine if it existed.

The trip began on May 30, when Columbus departed from Sanlucar, Spain, with six ships in his command. After a brief visit to Porto Santo, the small fleet headed to the Canary Islands once again for provisions. In the days that followed their departure, the ships reached an area of the Atlantic where there were virtually no winds. This resulted in a lack of progress, during which the crew became concerned about their lack of water. Fortunately, the winds picked up, and they were able to continue on.

July 31, 1498, proved to be a significant date, as the continent that would be known as South America was first spotted by Columbus when he arrived at Trinidad. He went ashore two days later at Punta del Arenal and explored the land that would become Venezuela. He concluded that this was, in fact, the hypothesized continent when he found that the Orinoco River contained fresh water, as opposed to salt water.

Columbus traveled north to Hispaniola and arrived on August 19. He found the settlement in rebellion, as the colonists maintained that he had lied to them about the economic potential of the area. The more devout Catholics among them were also bothered by his disregard for the baptism of the natives that he had originally cited as a goal of colonization.

Word of the colonists' discontent had already reached Spain by this point, and Ferdinand and Isabella were swift in their reaction. They sent a new governor to relieve Columbus of his duties and had him arrested. He then endured a humiliating trip back to Spain in chains. The king and queen restored his freedom shortly after his arrival. They refused to recognize his former authority, however, and his reputation was forever tarnished.

## The Fourth and Final Voyage

Columbus was ultimately able to persuade Ferdinand and Isabella to grant him permission for another voyage to the New World, despite no longer having any authority there. He sailed from Cadiz with four ships on May 11, 1502, along with his son Fernando. His primary intent was to find passage to the Indian Ocean, which would enable him to finally realize his goal of establishing a route to India.

The small group of ships made it across the Atlantic by mid-June. It was at this point that Columbus became aware of an impending hurricane and headed to Hispaniola. Francisco de Bobadilla, now acting governor, refused to allow Columbus to dock there, forcing him to seek shelter on the edge of the Rio Jaina. The governor also refused to heed Columbus's warning of the hurricane and embarked on his scheduled trip to Spain with thirty ships loaded with gold. The hurricane claimed twenty-nine of the ships, and approximately five hundred men, de Bobadilla among them, lost their lives.

After weathering the storm, Columbus continued on to Central America. He arrived at Puerto Castilla in the modern Honduras on August 14. For about two months, he traveled along the coast through what is now Nicaragua and Costa Rica, ultimately ending up in Panama in October.

Columbus remained in this area until April 16, 1503. Shipworms, which resided in the warm waters, had caused damage to his ships. As they passed through the vicinity of Cuba, yet another storm caused further damage. Columbus concluded that returning to Spain would not be possible, and they landed at Jamaica on June 25. They would remain stranded there for about a year, despite seeking help from Hispaniola. The current governor, Nicolas de Ovando y Caceres, refused to offer any support. Columbus won the favor of the Jamaican natives by accurately predicting the lunar eclipse that occurred on February 29, 1504, after which they provided the Spaniards with much-needed food.

Help ultimately arrived from Spain on June 29. The exhausted crew was finally able to embark on its return voyage. On November 7, Columbus returned to Spain, landing at Sanlucar. He would not return to the New World.

## Later Life

After returning from his final voyage, Columbus's health deteriorated. He suffered from what was believed to be gout, a severe form of arthritis, which gradually worsened. Several bouts of influenza followed as well.

As his condition worsened, Columbus pursued litigation against the Spanish crown. He insisted that he and his heirs were entitled to 10 percent of any revenue generated for the nation in the new colonies, according to the original agreement made between himself and the king and queen. The crown denied his claim, maintaining that his authority as governor had been revoked. The initial contract was nullified.

### Death and Legacy

Columbus passed away on May 20, 1506, in Valladolid, Spain. Beginning in 1508, his heirs engaged in lengthy litigation against the Spanish monarchy. The proceedings would come to be known as the *pleitos colombinos*, or Columbian lawsuits. In 1511, the court awarded Columbus's descendants recognition as viceroys as well as the original 10 percent of profits from the New World settlements. The family of Columbus was still not satisfied and continued to appeal to the court for several years.

The legal dispute was finally resolved through arbitration on June 28, 1536. It was agreed that the descendants of Columbus would retain the title Admiral of the Indies but would no longer be known as viceroys. The heirs were also granted sizable territory in Jamaica and Hispaniola, as well as an annual monetary payment.

Even after the agreement was reached, animosity continued between Columbus's descendants and the rulers of Spain. Minor lawsuits (the most notable of which occurred in 1537 and 1555) would be sporadically pursued by the line of Columbus through the late eighteenth century. None would have noteworthy ramifications.

Columbus holding an astrolabe, a device used to help identify stars and planets.

# Was Columbus a Hero or a Villain?

## Chapter Four

**A**s demonstrated throughout earlier chapters, Christopher Columbus led a highly adventurous life and accomplished a great deal. It cannot be denied that he had a lasting, long-term impact on societies and cultures all over the world. Columbus has been regarded by many as a true hero, possessing many qualities deserving of admiration. He met with a great deal of criticism during his lifetime, however, and a number of historians still maintain that he was more villainous than heroic.

## Arguments for Columbus as a Hero

Columbus endeavored to pursue great accomplishments at an early age. He grew up in a community characterized by turmoil and found himself involved in frequent skirmishes as a boy. He would later credit the challenges and difficult circumstances of his childhood with forcing him to develop a quick-witted nature and survival instincts. These would prove useful in many situations throughout his adult life.

## Persistence

Many scholars have expressed admiration for Columbus's persistent nature, which he demonstrated at a very young age. He did not receive a traditional education due to his father's insistence that he help out with the family business as soon as he was old enough to do so. Columbus spent several of his formative years in the service of his father, weaving wool, despite having no interest in this activity. He dreamed of a more adventurous lifestyle and refused to give up on it, as history would demonstrate.

Columbus did not allow his childhood illiteracy to limit his potential. He worked hard to learn a number of written languages, including Latin, Castilian, and Portuguese. This enabled him to study numerous written works, including *The Travels of Marco Polo* and the Bible, which would inspire him to seek great accomplishments. Also significant was Columbus's desire to express himself through writing, which would result in him keeping journals detailing his travels.

Further evidence of Columbus's persistent nature would be demonstrated when he sought sponsorship for his proposed westward voyage to reach the Indies. His initial attempt to convince King John II of Portugal to provide funding met with disapproval. The king's advisors ridiculed his plan, indicating that he had made numerous miscalculations. This was a major setback, as Columbus

Columbus's unique and distinctive signature.

had been counting on sponsorship from Portugal due to its rapid progress in exploration and colonization at the time. Columbus did not give up hope and would request a second audience with King John II. Despite his argument for the worthiness of his plan, it was again rejected.

Instead of abandoning his plan, Columbus began traveling around Europe, asking to be heard. He initially returned to his home of Genoa, where he was again denied support. This was followed by an equally unsuccessful appeal in Venice. He sent his brother Bartholomew to England, hoping to convince then-ruler King Henry VIII of the importance of his venture. This led to yet another refusal.

Columbus's ultimate success in attaining sponsorship from Spain has been highly documented. Less commonly known is the fact that support was not immediately offered.

After the initial meeting with Ferdinand and Isabella, Columbus was told that his proposal would be taken into consideration, but no commitment was made. Columbus would go on to make many appeals to Ferdinand and Isabella in the years to come. He followed them around the country, desperately requesting that they hear him out as he tried to present further evidence in favor of his plan. Court officials began to regard him as a nuisance, and he was often made fun of by those who regarded his intended voyage as ridiculous.

Admirers of Columbus are quick to point out that many people in his situation would have given up on the plan after several rejections. He did not do so, remaining steadfast in commitment to his goal and seeing it through to the end. Columbus's stubbornness and persistence ultimately resulted in the sponsorship of his voyage, which would change the course of history.

## Courage

When considering Columbus's heroic attributes, one can make a strong argument that he possessed great courage. This trait can probably be traced to his upbringing. As mentioned earlier, society in Genoa when Columbus was growing up was characterized by violence and strife. These circumstances likely forced Columbus to develop a brave demeanor as a necessity in day-to-day life.

At the time of his first voyage across the Atlantic Ocean, Europeans had not traveled very far west. Columbus proposed to venture very far into uncharted territory with no guaranteed assurance that he and his crew would be safe. Tales of giant sea monsters inhabiting unexplored parts of the Ocean Sea (as the Atlantic Ocean was called then) had been handed down from generation to generation. Some sailors on the initial voyage were fearful of the possibility that they may encounter such beasts.

Another risk involved in traveling into previously unexplored territory was the possibility of running out of food and water. Columbus was confident that land would be found, but he gambled on the probability that he had correctly calculated the distance around the earth. As it turned out, he had vastly underestimated this distance. If the area that would come to be known as the New World had been encompassed by water, the crew would have perished.

A further example of Columbus's bravery was demonstrated at the time of Ferdinand and Isabella's decision to sponsor his first voyage. He had made relatively few requests of them at their first meeting, and by all accounts, had appeared desperate for the opportunity to make his expedition. When the monarchs finally agreed to provide patronage in 1492, Columbus boldly increased his demands at the risk of offending them. He now required that he be granted the title of Admiral of the Ocean Sea if his voyage proved successful, as well as political power in any colonized lands. Furthermore, he modified his request to include a sizable portion of any monetary gains that would result from newly established colonies. Luckily for Columbus, the king and queen agreed to his terms.

Columbus demonstrated courage at numerous times in battle during his life. One example is his first major excursion aboard a ship, which took place around 1474. Columbus willingly joined an armed convoy whose stated intention was to rescue merchants who were ostensibly being threatened by the Ottomans. Although it turned out that the threat was not real, Columbus demonstrated courage and loyalty by putting himself in apparent harm's way.

The trip Columbus made to England and Ireland a few years later was as part of another armed convoy, delivering valuable merchandise to northern Europe through potentially hostile waters. Once again, Columbus moved forward despite the risk of harm or death. As it turned out, the threat this time was real, as many of Columbus's counterparts lost their lives in the violent battle, which ensued near Cape Saint Vincent.

Despite encountering little resistance from the native people on his first arrival in the New World, Columbus was engaged in battle on one occasion. An attempt at trading with the Ciguayo tribe on the island of Hispaniola angered the tribesmen, who fought back with arrows (leading Columbus to later name the inlet where this occurred the Bay of Arrows). Columbus and his men proved up to the challenge and emerged victorious.

Columbus would recount a tale of bravery, which occurred during his second exploration of the Americas. When he and his men went ashore on what is now Puerto Rico, they came upon a tribe that had taken two young boys captive from a rival tribe. The sailors intervened to rescue the two boys. After a brief battle, they were able to return the boys to their home.

Yet another example of courage in battle was demonstrated shortly after Columbus embarked on his fourth trans-Atlantic voyage. Prior to charting his westward course, Columbus learned that a Portuguese fort near Arzila, a Moroccan port, was under attack from the Moors. He headed there in May of 1502 and reportedly assisted with the rescue of the besieged soldiers.

## Strength of Conviction

Along with the aforementioned qualities of persistence and bravery, Columbus exemplified a good deal of faith and confidence in his beliefs. He studied accounts of the explorers who had lived before him as well as ancient philosophers. Once he made up his mind that the Far East could be reached by sailing west from Europe, he never wavered from his goal of making this a reality.

Columbus was steadfast in his faith in God throughout the countless trials he endured in his lifetime. He studied the Bible from the time he was able to read and would often quote from it in conversations and written communication. He maintained that he was a messenger from God and that the primary reason for his interest in exploring new territories was to spread Catholicism to those for whom the teachings of the Bible were unfamiliar.

Because of his professed faith, Columbus won support for his endeavors from the Pope, prior to attaining sponsorship. He would remain a friend of the Catholic Church throughout his lifetime and beyond. In the nineteenth century, Pope Pius IX recommended him for sainthood, although Columbus was never recognized as such.

When presenting his case for sponsorship to the Spanish monarchs, Columbus cited a Biblical verse (2 Esdras 6:42) as evidence that he could reach the Indies by sailing west. His interpretation of the verse was that it indicated that only one-seventh of the earth was covered by water, with the remainder being land. Although this would prove to be erroneous, it is a clear demonstration of the faith that Columbus maintained in the Catholic Bible.

Columbus further utilized his faith to gain the approval of Ferdinand and Isabella when they inquired of his long-term intentions regarding his voyage. He talked at great length about his intention to spread Catholicism around the world. In addition to evangelism, he promised them that he would use money that he received from the voyage to fund a large-scale effort to take back Jerusalem from the Muslims. He also indicated that he would finance the construction of a large church there upon the restoration of Catholic control.

In addition to his unwavering allegiance to the Catholic Church, Columbus was steadfast in his servitude to the Spanish crown. As he was being brought back to Spain in chains after his arrest for alleged tyranny in Hispaniola, the captain of the ship offered to release him from his restraints. Columbus declined the offer, despite the obvious discomfort that he was experiencing. He proclaimed that he would only agree to be released if it was by the direct order of the Spanish crown. He then endured the remainder of the trip back to Spain in shackles.

## Skill in Navigation

It can scarcely be argued that Columbus did not demonstrate considerable navigational skills on the evidence of his nautical successes. His friend Michele da Cuneo, who accompanied him on his second voyage, described him thus: "In my opinion, since Genoa was Genoa, there was never born a man so well equipped and expert in the art of navigation as the said lord Admiral." Despite not attending school as a child, he managed to teach himself the skills needed to maneuver through large bodies of water. This is impressive given the primitive instruments at his disposal.

Columbus demonstrated sound navigational skills during his initial voyage of 1492 when he guided his ships southward to pick up the "easterly trade winds" near the Canary Islands. As he had expected, the prevailing wind currents at this latitude blow from east to west with great

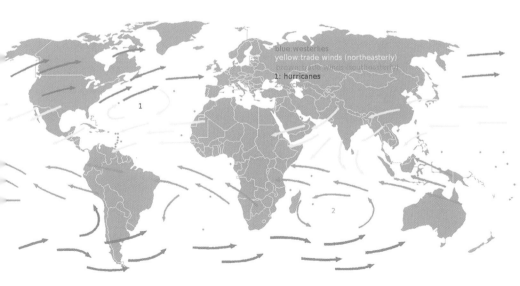

When traveling by sea in the fifteenth century, it was important to understand the predominant wind currents.

strength. The ships were thus able to cover a significant distance in a relatively short period of time.

Equally impressive was the foresight that Columbus demonstrated in charting his course back to Europe on the return trip. Whereas many sailors of the time would have simply reversed the original path and traveled east against the wind currents, he chose to take a northward trajectory. As he made his way to the North Atlantic, he was able to take advantage of the "westerly trade winds," which blew from west to east. This, in turn, made for a shorter and easier voyage home.

Columbus showed great proficiency in the early navigational system, referred to as "dead reckoning." This was the process of estimating the location of a ship by judging its speed over elapsed time and comparing it with a predetermined position. Of greater significance was the skill he demonstrated in celestial navigation. Columbus is considered a pioneer in the use of this method, which involved judging one's position based on calculated angles between astronomical bodies (such as stars, planets, or the moon) and the horizon. Columbus's ability to accurately chart his course using celestial navigation is a testament to his considerable effort and commitment to self-education.

## Charisma and Quick-Wittedness

Many accounts given by those who knew Columbus have described him as having a charming and warm personality, which endeared him to others. He was by all indications a "people person" in today's terminology. His natural ability to gain people's trust worked to his advantage in numerous instances on both sides of the Atlantic.

The most commonly cited example of how Columbus was able to influence others to his advantage was his eventual success in attaining the patronage of Ferdinand and Isabella. In the words of historian Milton Meltzer, "Columbus succeeded more on his salesmanship than his seamanship" in this endeavor. It is worth noting that Columbus and Isabella were around the same age, which by all indications was helpful in his winning her favor. Despite having to repeatedly argue against her advisors' claims that his proposed voyage was not a worthwhile investment, he ultimately won out.

The account of how Columbus was granted his first audience with the Spanish monarchs is an additional indication of his charisma. After leaving Portugal in despair and arriving in Spain with virtually no belongings, he and his son were forced to seek shelter at a monastery in Andalusia. At this point, Columbus was unknown in Spain. As luck would have it, the priest in charge of the monastery, Antonio de Marchena, happened to take an interest in astronomy (he was dubbed the "Astronomer Priest"). Columbus quickly picked up on this through initial conversation and shrewdly introduced his plan with an emphasis on his knowledge of astronomy. Columbus generated great enthusiasm in the priest, who strongly supported his planned voyage and influenced the Duke of Medina Celi to arrange for him to meet the king and queen.

Columbus was able to almost instantly attain the approval of the indigenous people, whom he first encountered when he arrived at San Salvador in 1492. He immediately surmised that they were a peaceful people but noted that several of them had scars. He demonstrated a concern for how they had sustained their injuries, which likely made them comfortable and accepting of him. He also delighted them by offering them small gifts, although by his own acknowledgement, they were of virtually no value in the eyes of the Europeans.

A remarkable example of Columbus's quick-wittedness has been recounted from the time that he and his crew were stranded on Jamaica toward the end of his fourth voyage. He had sent a crew member to Hispaniola by canoe to request help. No assistance was offered by Nicolas de Ovando y Caceres, the acting governor of Hispaniola, who reportedly hated Columbus. By this time, Columbus and his men were

Columbus amazes the natives of Jamaica by accurately predicting the lunar eclipse on February 29, 1504.

running out of provisions and were becoming desperate. The natives of the island seemed unconcerned by the plight of the crew. Columbus needed to act fast to convince them to feed and support this group of foreigners who had arrived on their land uninvited.

Utilizing his power of persuasion and aided by incredibly good luck, Columbus managed to win the approval of the Jamaican natives. Having studied charts that had been developed by Portuguese astronomer Abraham Zacuto, he believed that a lunar eclipse would be visible from the tropics on the evening of February 29, 1504. He boldly approached the natives and communicated to them that the moon would disappear from the sky. When the natives observed this occurrence on the evening that Columbus predicted, they were astounded and became convinced that Columbus possessed some supernatural power. They then willingly provided for him and his crew until help eventually arrived.

## Arguments for Columbus as a Villain

Many historians have painted Columbus in a positive light in the years between his lifetime and the present. In his own writings, he certainly purported to have only noble intentions. His son Fernando would describe him as "endowed with all the qualities that his great task required" in *The Life of the Admiral Christopher Columbus*. Others have viewed him very differently. Numerous arguments have been made for why he should be regarded as a villain.

# Amerigo Vespucci

AMERIC VESPVCE.

Amerigo Vespucci recognized the Western Hemisphere's lands as separate from Asia.

While Columbus is generally regarded as the explorer who "discovered the Americas," they would ultimately be named for Amerigo Vespucci (1454–1512). This Italian explorer made a number of voyages to South America between 1499 and 1502. He kept meticulous journals throughout his travels, which would all be published by 1504. He concluded, largely based on the length of the eastern coast of South America, that the lands discovered by Columbus were in fact part of a new continent of which Europeans had been unaware. Columbus maintained in his writings up until his death that he believed he had reached the Indies. Therefore, Vespucci is credited as the first person to identify the lands of the Western Hemisphere as a "New World." The Americas were subsequently named for him rather than Columbus.

## Cruelty

Columbus was known to all as a man with a strong, authoritative demeanor. As mentioned above, he was generally able to influence those around him to do what he desired. In writings by his supporters, this has been attributed to a warm and pleasant demeanor. His detractors paint a very different picture, indicating that he could have been remarkably cruel.

Upon his arrival at San Salvador in 1492, he immediately encountered native people, whom he surmised as being friendly. He would describe them thus in a letter to Ferdinand and Isabella: "They ought to make good and skilled servants, for they repeat very quickly whatever we say to them. I think they can very easily be made Christians, for they seem to have no religion. If it pleases our Lord, I will take six of them to Your Highnesses when I depart, in order that they may learn our language."

On the evidence of this writing, it appears that Columbus regarded the natives as being of a lowly stature. Despite the kindness that they showed to him and his crew, it appears by Columbus's own admission that he sought to subjugate them. As noted by author Robert Fuson, he would later write in his journal, "I could conquer the whole of them with 50 men, and govern them as I pleased."

Columbus would go on to enslave many native people throughout his voyages. In the year 1495 alone, he imprisoned approximately 1,500 members of the Arawak tribe and sent them to Spain to be sold into slavery. They were not well cared for on the trip, as evidenced by the deaths of over 200 of them en route.

A further example of Columbus's cruel and inhumane treatment of natives was the demand that he put on the inhabitants of Haiti. After taking over this island and claiming it for Spain, he forcibly put all of the natives over the age of fourteen to work searching for gold inland and panning for it in streams. Each was given a quota that they were expected to meet every three months. In the event that this quota was not met, the native was punished by having his or her hands cut off. As very little gold actually existed on the island, this penalty was exacted countless times. The natives thus lived in fear of the Spaniards. Those who attempted to flee from the colony were subsequently hunted and killed.

Another description of the cruelty exacted on the natives was given by Bartolome de las Casas, a priest who accompanied Columbus on his voyages, in his *Historia de las Indias*. He stated that Columbus and his men "thought nothing of knifing Indians by tens and twenties and of cutting slices off them to test the sharpness of their blades." He would go on to give an account of two Spaniards beheading two young native boys simply for their own amusement.

A statistic that many may find disturbing is the rapid reduction of the Arawak tribe on Haiti as a result of the Spanish takeover. Upon Columbus's arrival, it is estimated that this tribe numbered about 250,000. They were reduced to half of this number in the subsequent two years. The Arawaks quickly realized that they stood no hope of retaliation, as their primitive weapons could not compete with the Europeans' guns, swords, and armor. They eventually resorted to mass suicide to avoid the inevitable fate that awaited them at the hands of their captors. Some even made the difficult decision to feed poison to their infants. The cruel treatment of the natives continued even after Columbus left the area for good. As of 1550, only 500 Arawaks remained, and they were completely wiped out by 1650.

It may well be concluded that Columbus had little to no regard for the dignity of the indigenous inhabitants of the lands that he conquered. There are also some indications that he was cruel to the men under his command at times as well. For instance, upon arriving at Hispaniola during his third voyage, he discovered the rebellion of many of the Spanish settlers who felt he was a poor governor. He became angered at this and immediately ordered the hanging of several of his crewmembers as punishment for their disobedience.

On another occasion, Columbus is said to have threatened his entire crew. Prior to their return to Spain after the first voyage, it was speculated by some that they had not in fact reached the lands of the Indies that Columbus had intended as their destination. Columbus, having already written the Spanish monarchs about the success of the voyage and fearing ridicule, ordered the entire crew to take an oath. They reportedly agreed to state with certainty to anyone who asked that the lands they discovered were part of the Indies. Columbus vowed to cut out the tongue of anyone who broke this oath.

## Inept as Governor

Supporters of Columbus have lavished great praise on him for his sailing and navigational aptitude. It is clear that he possessed a great degree of self-confidence and seemed to believe he could be successful in anything he undertook. This included serving as viceroy and governor of the new settlements that came about as a result of his exploration. Ferdinand and Isabella, impressed by the success of his initial voyage, were quick to grant him this authority. As it turned out, they lived to regret this decision.

Although many of the Spanish settlers were complicit in the tyranny and cruelty exacted by Columbus on the native people, a number of them found it horrific and completely unnecessary. Bartolome de las Casas, sickened by what he observed, wrote extensively of the mistreatment and would become an outspoken critic of Columbus. He would ultimately be given the title "Protector of the Indians" by the Spanish crown after Columbus's time to ensure that the natives in the colonies were treated kindly.

An early indication of Columbus's ineptitude as governor came about after he left thirty-nine Spaniards in charge of the settlement of La Navidad. He gave them little guidance and left them to their own devices while he returned to Spain. The colonists had observed the disregard Columbus had for the native people and quickly began to mistreat them. Despite being vastly outnumbered, the colonists assumed that they were not in danger of retaliation, owing to the peaceful nature of the tribal people.

Eventually, the natives became angered by the way they were being treated by these uninvited foreigners. The Spanish men became lonely, due to the fact that no women had traveled with them from Europe, and attempted to take the native women by force as their mistresses. This was reportedly seen by the natives as the most offensive behavior exhibited by the settlers, and it finally angered them to the point of violence.

Columbus assumed that the men he had left in charge of La Navidad would easily be able to overpower the natives in the event of an uprising. When he finally returned to Hispaniola during his second voyage, he was astounded to find that the natives had destroyed the fort that had been built there, killing eleven of the settlers in the process.

The founding of the settlement of La Isabella is regarded as an example of poor planning and leadership on the part of Columbus. In the wake of the destruction of La Navidad, Columbus hurriedly established this settlement on the eastern coast of Haiti. He based its location on an erroneous report that there was gold in the area and once again left a group of settlers with little direction as he moved on to other areas.

The ultimate demise of La Isabella was largely due to its poor location. A hurricane struck the area in 1494, then another in 1495. Considering the awareness that Columbus had exhibited of weather patterns in the Atlantic Ocean (such as his adept utilization of the tradewinds to minimize the length of journeys both westward and eastward), it has been speculated that he should have been aware of La Isabella's potential for dangerous weather.

As the settlers were unprepared for the storms, many perished. Those that survived were frustrated and disillusioned. Disease ran rampant through the settlement, and lack of food further complicated matters. At one point, a settler named Bernal de Pisa led a poorly planned mutiny with the goal of stealing ships to return to Spain. La Isabella was ultimately abandoned in 1496.

The most prevalent testament to the lack of faith the Spanish settlers had in Columbus as a leader came about when he returned to Hispaniola on his third trip to the Western Hemisphere. He discovered that the colonists under his authority as governor had become angered by what they perceived as empty promises he had made about the gold waiting to be discovered.

It must be noted that Columbus was beginning to waver in his belief that he could effectively govern the colony at this point. His physical stamina was wearing down due to arthritis, and he was gradually losing his eyesight. As a result, he made a request of Spain in October 1499 that a commissioner be sent to assist him in the oversight of Hispaniola.

By this time, Spain had already been notified of a general lack of faith in Columbus as leader and had dispatched Francisco de Bobadilla to Hispaniola to investigate. It was understood that Bobadilla would depose Columbus as viceroy and governor of Hispaniola if he felt this was warranted. He arrived at the colony while Columbus was away investigating other islands and heard numerous complaints from the settlers. He was reportedly horrified by the accounts of torture and inhumane treatment of both natives and insubordinate colonists by Columbus.

In addition to the examples of cruelty outlined earlier in this chapter, Bobadilla heard a testimony that a woman had been punished for stating that Columbus was of lowly birth by having her tongue cut out and being forced to walk naked through the colony. He also learned of the brutal dismemberment of natives who had attempted to revolt and how their mutilated bodies had been paraded along the streets. Bobadilla noted that even Columbus's supporters would acknowledge that his government was tyrannical and merciless.

When Bobadilla relayed his findings to the king and queen, they concluded that Columbus was entirely inept as a leader. They had him arrested and brought back to Spain, where he was kept in prison for over a month. Bobadilla assumed the role of governor of Hispaniola, much to the relief of the colonists and remaining natives.

## Dishonesty and Manipulation

Columbus was often praised for his warm and inviting demeanor. This served him well in his endeavors to win support and influence people in pursuit of his goals. While this has been cited as a heroic quality, detractors would indicate that Columbus often used it for villainous purposes.

Columbus presented himself as a highly devout Catholic throughout his life. He clearly used this to his advantage in gaining support for his first voyage, claiming that he fully intended to introduce Christianity to all unenlightened people with whom he came in contact over the course of his travels. This won him the support of the Pope and certainly helped him to gain support from Spain. Ferdinand and Isabella were impressed by his stated intention to spread

Catholicism. Equally intriguing was his promise to use money that he received from the expedition to fund efforts to recapture Jerusalem from the Ottomans.

His stated commitment to evangelism worked to his advantage, as his voyage was funded by Ferdinand and Isabella and fully supported by the Catholic Church. It would quickly become clear that Columbus actually regarded the conversion of the natives as a goal of little to no importance. Upon his arrival in the New World, he quickly took several of them prisoner. Although he maintained in his communication with the Spanish monarchs that he planned to Christianize them, it has been made clear that he went on to treat them much differently.

Scholars have cited Columbus's claim to be the first person in his fleet to spot land in the west on his first voyage as a glaring example of his willingness to lie and cheat for his personal gain. As part of the original agreement made between the Spanish monarchs and the crew, Ferdinand and Isabella had requested that they be notified of who amongst the crew saw land first. They promised to award to this man a royal pension for the remainder of his life.

The first announcement of a land sighting was made on October 12, 1492, at approximately 2:00 a.m. Juan Rodriguez Bermeo, who was stationed on the *Pinta*, shouted "Land! Land!" Martin Alonso Pinzon, who was acting captain of the *Pinta*, maintained that he immediately fired a cannon to signal to Columbus that land had been spotted.

Columbus initially made no argument that Bermeo was the first to spot land. Much to the disdain of Bermeo and other crewmembers, he later reported having seen a light to the west about four hours prior to being notified of Bermeo's claim. He maintained that the movement of this light indicated that it was being carried by humans. He therefore cited this as evidence of land and claimed the pension promised by the monarchs.

In recent years, some scholars have theorized that Columbus may have known much more than he let on regarding the layout of the world, keeping his knowledge a secret so that he could claim to "discover" new areas of which he was actually aware. It is well known that he visited England and Ireland prior to developing his plan to reach the Indies by sailing west. Some believe that he may have heard the tales of Leif Eriksson and the Viking colonies that had been briefly established on North America. If this were true, it can be reasonably concluded that Columbus may have suspected that there were significant lands across the Ocean Sea, waiting to be explored.

Modern debate has led to more speculation on the degree to which Columbus may have had prior knowledge of the New World. Some historians have suggested the possibility that he came by a "secret map," which he followed in the hope of attaining riches and glory. Despite his indicated intentions of evangelizing to those in need of enlightenment and establishing a safe trade route between Europe and East Asia, Columbus's actions while in the New World suggest that he was highly motivated to discover gold. This is particularly evidenced by his impatience with the natives when they failed to furnish gold after being ordered to do so. Such behavior could indicate that someone had led him to believe he was headed for an area filled with riches.

Critics of Columbus also point to his own writings as evidence that he may not have been entirely forthcoming when discussing details of his journey. For example, while on his first voyage westward, he wrote in his journal that after he left the Canary Islands, he sailed against the current for a good deal of time. It is now known that at this latitude, the trade winds blow from east to west. In fact, the relative speed with which Columbus made it across the Atlantic indicates that he must have had the wind at his back. It has been postulated that Columbus could not have unknowingly made this written error, leading to the conclusion that he was deliberately trying to mislead anyone who attempted to follow in his path.

## Spread of Disease

One of the most far-reaching, though unintended, negative effects of the voyages of Columbus to the Western Hemisphere is the introduction of diseases that resulted. Columbus has frequently been criticized as being the cause of more lost lives than Adolf Hitler. His aforementioned willingness to kill and maim natives is in large part to blame for this. The number of deaths caused by diseases exchanged between Europe and the Americas is even more staggering.

As is well documented, Europe had seen its share of diseases throughout the centuries, prior to the time of Columbus. Over time, Europeans developed immunity, or physical tolerance, for common illnesses. The same was true of the native inhabitants of the Western Hemisphere.

Diseases and illness were the cause of many deaths in Columbus's time.

Columbus claims more land for Spain.

There were many differences between the diseases of the two cultures, with the result that neither the natives nor the Europeans were readily able to endure each other's illnesses.

Statistically, the most deadly European disease introduced to the Americas was smallpox. It has been estimated that the disease caused a staggering 80 to 90 percent fatality rate among the Native American people from the time of Columbus's first voyage through the sixteenth century. It is believed that the smallpox epidemic began in Hispaniola when Columbus brought his second group of colonists there in 1493. As these colonists were equally susceptible to the diseases of the natives, two-thirds of their number succumbed to illness in the ensuing year.

New diseases were also spread to Europe as a result of the colonization of the Americas. Several of the men who served Columbus on the first voyage reportedly contracted syphilis from the natives. When they returned to Europe, a number of them were enlisted in support of King Charles VIII of France during his 1495 invasion of Italy. This resulted in the disease being spread across a sizable portion of Europe, with the ultimate effect of over five million deaths.

European and American history can scarcely be discussed without mention of Christopher Columbus and his pioneering voyages across the Atlantic Ocean. His proponents and critics continue to debate how he should be viewed, in light of his intentions and actions. As with many other significant historical figures, it is unlikely that this debate will soon come to an end, due to the overwhelming wealth of evidence that has been compiled to support both arguments.

Columbus took a keen interest in cartography throughout his life.

# Later Effects of Columbus

## Chapter Five

The lasting impact of Christopher Columbus on Western culture has been significant. In the years that followed his voyages, many European explorers from various countries were inspired to venture further into the continents of the Western Hemisphere. A number of colonies were established, and many evolved into independent nations. Cultures in North and South America have grown and developed quickly in the past five hundred years, and they can all trace their lineage either directly or indirectly to Columbus.

## Explorers After Columbus

One significant effect Columbus had on later history was his influence on later explorers. He set out to find a new route to the Indies—a goal that he would not accomplish in his lifetime. Other adventurous sailors would attempt to find new routes and lands with varying degrees of success.

## Ferdinand Magellan

Ferdinand Magellan was a Portuguese explorer who lived from about 1480 to 1521. He followed in Columbus's footsteps in seeking a western route to the Indies. While it cannot be confirmed, there has been speculation that he may have met Columbus as a young boy when Columbus was residing in Portugal and seeking the patronage of King John II.

After Columbus failed to find the western passage to the Indies, Spain continued to put forth effort to achieve this goal. King Charles I, who would succeed Ferdinand and Isabella, commissioned Magellan to travel west and seek passage to the Spice Islands. He was placed in command of five ships, which he guided on a southward course through the Atlantic Ocean, beginning on August 10, 1519. They gradually made their way to the southern tip of South America by November 1 and sailed inland through a channel that is now known as the Strait of Magellan. They reached the Pacific Ocean on November 28.

Magellan and his crew ultimately arrived at the tribal kingdom of Mactan, which is located in the Philippines. There, he was killed in battle on April 27, 1521. His crew continued on through the Indian Ocean and ultimately returned to Spain.

Ferdinand Magellan ultimately succeeded in reaching the Indies by voyaging west.

Magellan's expedition succeeded in achieving the original goal Columbus had in that they reached the Indies by sailing west. More significantly, it resulted in the first complete trip around the world. The completion of the voyage was ultimately credited to Juan Sebastian Elcano, who assumed command of the fleet upon Magellan's death.

## Hernán Cortés

Hernán Cortés was a Spanish explorer who traveled to North America in the sixteenth century. He arrived at modern Mexico in 1519 with an army of over five hundred men and several cannons. He gradually made his way through the mainland, conquering small groups of the native Aztec civilization. Many of them chose to join him rather than be killed.

Cortés arrived at Tenochtitlan, the Aztec capital, on November 8. He took Aztec leader Moctezuma II hostage and assumed control over the capital. Moctezuma was killed in a skirmish the following year, but the remaining Aztecs temporarily drove out Cortés and his men. Cortés was granted more men and supplies and ultimately reconquered Tenochtitlan. On August 13, 1521, Cortés captured Cuauhtemoc, the successor to Moctezuma. He claimed all of Mexico for Spain at this point and assumed the role of governor of the colony.

Cortés is referred to as a conquistador (or conqueror) as he forcibly overpowered a preexisting civilization. Like Columbus, he professed to have the goal of spreading

Hernán Cortés, conqueror of the Aztec civilization.

Christianity to new lands, but he ultimately showed little compassion toward the indigenous people with whom he came in contact. Historians credit him with beginning the large-scale Spanish colonization of the Western Hemisphere, which would continue for years to come.

## Colonization of the United States

The modern United States of America are often described as resulting from the discovery of Columbus. One of the first European colonies in this area was established by British settlers in 1607 at Jamestown, Virginia. The Plymouth colony in Massachusetts was established soon after, in 1620.

Throughout the seventeenth and eighteenth centuries, the southern part of the United States was gradually being settled by the Spanish as they branched out from Mexico into what would become Florida and the southwestern continental United States. French exploration took place, beginning in present-day eastern Canada before moving inland toward the Great Lakes and south along the Mississippi River. Meanwhile, colonists continued to arrive from England along the East Coast, culminating in the establishment of thirteen colonies in which 2.5 million people resided by the time of the American Revolution.

Since achieving independence, the United States has continued to grow and expand in both area and population. It is currently the third most populated nation in the world, with a total number of people in excess of 325 million. Its current area is 3.8 million square miles (9.8 million square kilometers).

# The Legacy of Columbus

The influence attributed to Christopher Columbus on Western culture can be seen at the number of places in existence today that are named after him. The nation of Colombia, located in South America, is the largest. The District of Columbia, capital of the United States, is also named for Columbus. There are cities named for Columbus in many states, including Georgia, Mississippi, New York, Ohio, and South Carolina.

The Canadian province of British Columbia derives part of its name from Columbus. Similarly named is the Columbia River, which flows through the province as well as the states of Washington and Oregon. Also worthy of note is Columbia University in New York City.

## Some Common Misconceptions

One erroneous belief that has been widespread for many years is the idea that Christopher Columbus was the first person in history to believe that the earth was round. According to this legend, Europeans in the fifteenth century thought that the earth was flat and ridiculed Columbus for disputing this obvious "fact." He therefore had difficulty in obtaining sponsorship for his voyage because his contemporaries thought that by sailing west, he would reach the edge of the world and fall off into space.

The truth is that knowledge of the spherical shape of the earth had been established by the ancient Greeks. By the time Columbus sought to make his voyage, it was common knowledge that the earth was round. Those who ridiculed his plan did so in the belief that he had underestimated the size of the earth.

Another common misconception is that Columbus was the first non-native person to set foot in what is now the United States of America. This seems to stem from the designation of Columbus as the "Discoverer of America." As has been shown earlier in this book, most of the areas that he explored were islands in the Caribbean Sea. He was never actually in any part of the modern United States, although he did visit the mainlands of South America and Central America.

## Columbus Day

Columbus Day has been a long-standing national holiday in the United States as well as many other nations. It was established to celebrate the anniversary of Columbus's arrival at San Salvador in October of 1492. It is now observed in the United States on the second Monday in October each year.

The American tradition of celebrating the arrival of Columbus can be traced back to its three-hundredth anniversary in 1792, when the United States was in its infancy. A large celebration was held in New York City that year. In 1892, President Benjamin Harrison encouraged the people of the nation to celebrate the four-hundredth anniversary of Columbus's landing with enthusiasm.

The first official use of the term "Columbus Day" occurred in 1905. That year, the state of Colorado adopted it as a state holiday. It would not be established as a national holiday until 1934. Since then, it has been observed with the closing

Modern replicas of the *Niña*, *Pinta*, and *Santa María*.

of schools, post offices, and many businesses throughout the country.

## Indigenous Peoples' Day

Very different opinions have formed of Christopher Columbus since his voyages. While the celebration of Columbus Day has been indicative of his status as a hero in the eyes of many people, others have taken issue with this viewpoint. The movement to change the name of the holiday to Indigenous Peoples' Day is a result of modern disdain for Columbus and his treatment of the natives who preceded him in the New World.

The first observance of Indigenous Peoples' Day occurred in 1992 in Berkeley, California. This coincided with the five-hundredth anniversary of Columbus's arrival in the Americas. Santa Cruz, California, adopted the name change two years later. In the past decade, it has spread to a number of cities throughout the United States.

Discussion of a replacement for Columbus Day in the United States can be traced back to 1977. In that year, the United Nations held the International Conference on Discrimination Against Indigenous Populations in the Americas. In the years to follow, Native American groups would hold demonstrations, most notably in Boston, Massachusetts, to protest the celebration of Columbus Day.

The First Continental Conference on Five Hundred Years of Indian Resistance took place in Quito, Ecuador, in 1990. A number of Native American groups were represented at the conference in anticipation of the five-hundredth anniversary of Columbus's voyage two years later. A general commitment was established to promote unity among people of all races and backgrounds in 1992.

San Francisco, California, planned a massive "Quincentennial Jubilee" for Columbus Day in 1992. As part of the celebration, detailed replicas of the *Niña*, *Pinta*, and *Santa María* were built and planned to sail into San Francisco Bay in a reenactment of the arrival of Columbus. The celebration was heavily protested by an organization of Native Americans referred to as the Bay Area Indian Alliance.

Since the establishment of Indigenous Peoples' Day in Berkeley, numerous municipalities and institutions throughout the United States have elected to either rename Columbus Day or decline its celebration altogether. The states of Alaska, Hawaii, and Oregon do not recognize any such holiday. South Dakota has adopted Native American Day as an alternative. US cities that have replaced Columbus Day with Indigenous Peoples' Day include Los Angeles, California; Oberlin, Ohio; and Bangor, Maine.

## Further Protests

In recent years, protest of the celebration of Christopher Columbus has continued to mount in various communities of the United States. In 2017, a great deal of controversy was raised in New York City over the possibility of removing a statue of Columbus sculpted by Gaetano Russo in Columbus Circle. Within the same year, a well-known monument to Columbus in Baltimore, Maryland, was severely vandalized. Similar controversy has been noted with regard to a statue of Columbus in Long Branch, New Jersey. The community's large Hispanic population has expressed their disdain for Columbus. As of this writing, they are lobbying to have the statue moved out of the area.

## Conclusion

Christopher Columbus was a figure of major significance to world history. His impact on the development of culture throughout the Western Hemisphere has been widespread. Many diverse populations can trace their histories to the arrival of Columbus in the Americas in one way or another.

He has been celebrated as a heroic figure by many historians since his voyages. His repeated persistence in the face of adversity has been a much-celebrated trait. He demonstrated great courage throughout his life and was able to make difficult decisions with conviction. His navigational skills have been frequently applauded. The Catholic Church was willing to support him based on the strength of his faith.

A statue of Columbus in Providence, Rhode Island.

Columbus has also had his share of critics throughout history, who have espoused the belief that he was more villainous than heroic. They have pointed out his often cruel, demeaning treatment of the people who initially inhabited the areas he colonized. His inability to effectively govern the colonies he established has earned him further criticism. Numerous indications of his manipulative, dishonest, and arrogant nature have been put forth. He has also been blamed for the spread of diseases across cultures and the deaths that resulted.

To summarize, Christopher Columbus has been, and continues to be, the subject of great controversy. He achieved a great deal in his lifetime and significantly influenced the course of history. Whether he did so for better or for worse is a matter of opinion to be decided by each individual.

**admiral** The commander-in-chief of a fleet of ships.

**caravel** A small, highly maneuverable sailing ship developed by the Portuguese to explore along the West African coast and into the Atlantic Ocean.

**cartography** The science or art of making maps.

**coat of arms** A shield with symbols and figures that represent a family, person, group or other organization.

**convoy** A group of ships traveling together.

**dead reckoning** The process of calculating one's current position by using a previously determined position and advancing that position based on estimated speeds over elapsed time and course.

**heathen** Someone who does not belong to an accepted religion.

**Indies** In Columbus's time, the area of the world encompassing Southeast Asia and India.

**missionary** A person sent by a church into an area to carry on evangelism or other activities.

**monarch** A person who reigns over a kingdom or empire, such as a king or queen.

# Glossary

**monastery** The building where monks live while practicing their religion.

**Ocean Sea** The area covered by water that in the time of Columbus was believed to cover the area between Europe and the East Indies.

**patron** A person who uses wealth or influence to help an individual, institution, or cause.

**tradewinds** Winds that blow almost constantly in one direction.

**viceroy** The governor of a country or province who rules as the representative of a king or sovereign.

## 1451
The likely birth year of Columbus.

## 1474–5
Columbus travels to Chios in first major
sea excursion.

## 1476
Columbus travels to England and possibly Iceland.

## 1477
Columbus takes up residence in Lisbon.

## 1485
Columbus is denied support by King John II
of Portugal.

## 1492
Columbus gains patronage of King Ferdinand and
Queen Isabella of Spain, makes first voyage across
the Atlantic.

**1493**

Columbus returns to Spain, is named Admiral of the Ocean Sea, makes second voyage.

**1498**

Columbus makes third voyage, discovers South America.

**1500**

Columbus is deposed as governor of Hispaniola, arrested, and forcibly brought to Spain.

**1502**

Columbus makes fourth voyage.

**1503**

Columbus is stranded on Jamaica.

**1504**

Columbus returns to Spain.

## Books

Bergreen, Laurence. *Columbus: The Four Voyages, 1492–1504*. Westminster, UK: Penguin Books, 2012.

Hinckley, Clark B. *Christopher Columbus: A ManAmong the Gentiles*. Salt Lake City, UT: Deseret Book Co., 2014.

Kennedy, Alexander. *Columbus: Lies of a New World*. CreateSpace Independent Publishing Platform, 2016.

Loewen, James W. *Lies My Teacher Told Me About Christopher Columbus: What Your History Books Got Wrong*. New York: The New Press, 2014.

Morison, Samuel Eliot. *Admiral of the Ocean Sea: A Life of Christopher Columbus*. New York City: Little, Brown and Company, 1991.

Ortiz, Rafael. *Christopher Columbus the Hero: Defending Columbus from Modern Day Revisionism*. CreateSpace Independent Publishing Platform, 2017.

## Websites

**The Ages of Exploration: Christopher Columbus**
http://exploration.marinersmuseum.org/subject/
christopher-columbus
This site contains facts about Columbus and other
explorers over different points in history.

**Biography: Christopher Columbus**
http://biography.com/people/christopher-
columbus-9254209
This site contains numerous videos pertaining to
Columbus's life.

**History: Christopher Columbus**
http://history.com/topics/exploration/christopher-
columbus
The History Channel's site, featuring documentaries and
videos about Columbus.

Barden, Renardo. *The Discovery of America: Opposing Viewpoints.* San Diego, CA: Greenhaven Press, Inc., 1989.

Bruun, Erik, and Jay Crosby, eds. *Our Nation's Archive: The History of the United States in Documents.* New York: Black Dog & Leventhal Publishers, Inc., 1999.

Colon, Fernando. *The Life of the Admiral Christopher Columbus by His Son Ferdinand.* New Brunswick, NJ: Rutgers University Press, 1959.

Crow, John A. *The Epic of Latin America.* Los Angeles, CA: University of California Press, 1992.

Cummins, John. *The Voyage of Christopher Columbus: Columbus' Own Journal of Discovery.* New York: St. Martin's Press, 1992.

de Las Casas, Bartolome. *Historia de las Indias.* Madrid: Ginestra, 1875-76.

Dyson, John. *Columbus: For Gold, God and Glory: In Search of the Real Christopher Columbus.* New York: Simon & Schuster, 1991.

# Bibliography

Fernandez-Armesto, Felipe. *Columbus.* Oxford: Oxford University Press, 1991.

Formisano, Luciano, ed. *Letters from a New World: Amerigo Vespucci's Discovery of America.* New York: Marsilio, 1992.

Freedman, Russell. *Who was First? Discovering the Americas.* New York: Clarion Books, 2007.

Fuson, Robert H., translator. *The Log of Christopher Columbus.* Camden, ME: International Marine Publishing Company, 1987.

Gallagher, Carole. *Christopher Columbus and the Discovery of the New World.* New York: Simon & Schuster, Inc., 2000.

Jones, Mary Ellen. *Christopher Columbus and His Legacy: Opposing Viewpoints Series.* San Diego, CA: Greenhaven Press, Inc., 1992.

Kubal, Timothy. *Cultural Movements and Collective Memory: Christopher Columbus and the Rewriting of the National Origin Myth.* New York: Palgrave Macmillan, 2009.

Lunenfeld, Marvin. *"Christopher Columbus."* World Book Encyclopedia. Cleveland, OH: Scott Fetzer Company, 2008.

Meltzer, Milton. *Columbus and the World Around Him.* New York: Franklin Watts, 1990.

Miller, Gordon. *Voyages: To the New World and Beyond.* Seattle: WA: University of Washington Press, 2011.

Morison, Samuel Eliot. *Christopher Columbus, Mariner.* Boston, MA: Little, Brown and Company, 1955.

——. *Journals and Other Documents on the Life and Voyages of Christopher Columbus.* New York: The Heritage Press, 1963.

Phillips, William D., Jr, and Carla Rahn Phillips. *The Worlds of Christopher Columbus.* Cambridge, UK: Cambridge University Press, 1993.

Scavone, Daniel, contributing author. *Explorers.* Pasadena, CA: Salem Press, Inc., 1998.

Sundel, Al. *Christopher Columbus and the Age of Exploration in World History.* New Jersey: Enslow Publishers, Inc., 2002.

Page numbers in **boldface** are illustrations.

# Index

**Christopher Brink** has a Master of Science in Education from Alfred University. He resides in western New York State with his wife, Holly, and their three pets. He has worked in the field of education for ten years. He enjoys music, studying history, and traveling.